A TIME FOR EVERYTHING

for 8 - part mixed choir

Text: Ole Dalgaard
Music: Bo Holten

Semplice

A TIME FOR EVERYTHING

A time for joy.
A time for sorrow.
A time for heartbreaks, time for schemes.
A time to tear, to dare tomorrow.
The time we've got, the time it seems.

A time to fight.
A time to follow.
A time to search, to lose your mind.
A time to bat, to beat them hollow.
The time we thought we'd left behind.

A time to sow.
A time for reaping.
A time for pain a Folly be.
A time to wrath, a time for weeping.
The time we lost eternally.

Ole Dalgaard